TOP YOUTUBE STARS™

TYLER OAKLEY

LGBTQ+ Activist with More than
660 MILLION VIEWS

ANITA LOUISE MCCORMICK

rosen publishing's
rosen central®

New York

Published in 2020 by The Rosen Publishing Group, Inc.
29 East 21st Street, New York, NY 10010

Library of Congress Cataloging-in-Publication Data

Names: McCormick, Anita Louise, author.
Title: Tyler Oakley: LGBTQ+ Activist with More than 660 Million Views / Anita Louise McCormick.
Description: First edition. | New York : Rosen Central, 2020. | Series: Top YouTube stars | Audience: Grades 5–8. | Includes bibliographical references and index.
Identifiers: LCCN 2018053051| ISBN 9781725346222 (library bound) | ISBN 9781725346215 (paperback)
Subjects: LCSH: Oakley, Tyler, 1989– —Juvenile literature. | YouTube (Electronic resource)—Biography—Juvenile literature. | Actors—United States—Biography—Juvenile literature. | Celebrities—United States—Biography—Juvenile literature.
Classification: LCC PN1992.9236.O25 M35 2020 | DDC 791.092 [B]—dc23
LC record available at https://lccn.loc.gov/2018053051

Manufactured in the United States of America

On the cover: Tyler Oakley, YouTube star and advocate for the LGBTQ+ community, arrives at the 2016 Streamy Awards in Beverly Hills, California.

CONTENTS

On October 13, 2018, Tyler Oakley went to the Minneapolis Convention Center to claim the Human Rights Campaign's Visibility Award. The Human Rights Campaign (HRC) is the largest group in the United States that advocates for LGBTQ+ rights. This award recognized Oakley for his efforts to use his talent and visibility as a YouTube star to improve the lives of LGBTQ+ people.

In his acceptance speech, Oakley thanked the HRC for the award and talked about how important it is for LGBTQ+ youth to see people like themselves in the media. He said, "My lack of queer role models and lack of queer-positive representation in the media made me fear the worst while I was being outed. Positive representation and visibility can help clear away the mysterious cloud that feels like a looming thunderstorm."

While advocating for LGBTQ+ visibility is important to Oakley, his fan base goes far beyond the LGBTQ+ community. Most of the videos Oakley posts on his YouTube channel are fun and chatty. He loves to talk about celebrities, food, pop culture, music festivals, and things that are going on in his life. Through his years as a vlogger, Oakley has collaborated with many other vloggers, bringing new fans to his, as well as their, YouTube channels. While it does not happen as often today as it did years ago, Oakley sometimes gets messages from YouTube viewers saying that he is the first gay person they ever had the opportunity to know.

Tyler Oakley is part of the first wave of celebrities who became famous by posting videos on YouTube. He has more than seven and a half million followers on YouTube and more than six million followers on Twitter. He is the winner of a long list of awards, including the Streamy Awards, *Hollywood Reporter's* Top 25 Digital Stars, and a

Throughout his career as a YouTube vlogger, Tyler Oakley has been active in causes such as advocating for LGBTQ+ rights and encouraging young people to vote.

Teen Choice Award. In 2017, Oakley was selected by *Forbes* for their 30 under 30 achievement award. In 2018, he won the Human Rights Campaign's Visibility Award for his work. Since he first set up a channel on YouTube, Oakley's videos have helped many LGBTQ+ people feel accepted and find the courage to come out.

As with many YouTube vlogger celebrities, Oakley's fame is international. Hannah Ellis-Petersen, writer for the UK newspaper *The Guardian,* says:

Oakley is among the new generation of celebrities who have made their name entirely through YouTube. Posting videos of themselves from their bedrooms, discussing everything from pop culture and shopping to their own sexuality and mental health, teenagers across the world obsessively consume the content, interacting with the internet stars through comments, Twitter and Snapchat. It is a highly profitable occupation–some of the biggest You-Tube celebrities, Oakley included–are thought to earn six figure salaries through sponsorship and advertising alone.

The world of YouTube and vlogging has changed dramatically since Tyler Oakley first decided to post a video on YouTube. In a 2015 interview with Kevin Fallon of the Daily Beast, Oakley said, "When I started doing it in 2007, nobody had a million views. The most subscribed person I remember when I first started might have had 40,000 subscribers or something. Now you can really be in charge of your own trajectory."

Oakley has indeed taken charge of the trajectory of his career. And it has taken him to places that neither he nor his family ever could have imagined.

CHAPTER ONE

Growing Up in Michigan

Tyler Oakley was born on March 22, 1989, in Jackson, Michigan. Jackson is a small town located near Ann Arbor, Michigan. When Tyler was a toddler, his parents decided to get a divorce. During the divorce, his mother, Jackie Oakley, won primary custody of Tyler. Tyler's older sister, Codi, went to live with their father.

TWO LARGE FAMILIES

Both of Tyler's parents remarried within a few years of their divorce. Jackie married Ken, who then became Tyler's stepfather. During his childhood, Tyler lived in two households. In all, he had eleven step and half brothers and sisters. Tyler was one of six children who lived with his mother and stepfather. When Tyler was six years old, his mother and stepfather moved to Okemos, Michigan.

Jackie and Ken were poor, but they did their best to provide for their children. While they could not afford things some other

Tyler Oakley has a close relationship with his mother, Jackie Oakley. Jackie has always been there for Tyler to offer support and encouragement.

families had, they found ways to create their own fun at home. At an early age, Tyler found that he enjoyed entertaining. He and the other children in the household enjoyed putting on shows for their parents. They came up with stories and then acted out the parts. When Tyler was in kindergarten, he had the opportunity to be in a class play, *Teddy Bear's Picnic*. Tyler had a speaking part and sang in the choir.

Since the family did not have much money, Tyler and his stepbrothers and stepsisters came up with many ways to earn money to buy the things they wanted. They ran lemonade stands, shoveled snow and driveways, and did odd jobs. With so many children in the family, Tyler became self-sufficient and did things such as packing his own lunch for school and arranging carpools when he needed a ride. Later in life, Oakley said these experiences helped him to learn about being an entrepreneur, as well as how to collaborate with others. Those skills came in handy when Oakley decided to start his own YouTube channel and make vlogging into a career.

While Tyler knew that his mother and stepfather loved and accepted him, Tyler's life was not always easy. Tyler knew that his father was trying to get primary custody, and he did not want that to happen. Tyler's father had religious beliefs that made him a stricter parent than Jackie. Tyler was always worried that he would have to leave Jackie and Ken and move in with his father. The stress of living with two families and not knowing if he would have to move made Tyler feel anxious. He used food to help him deal with his anxiety and became overweight. Being overweight, along with having a bowl haircut, made it hard for Tyler to be popular at school. He was often teased and bullied by other students.

COMING TO TERMS WITH BEING GAY

While Oakley was still in elementary school, he started to realize that he was gay. At first, he kept it to himself. He was afraid of what other people might think if they found out. Then one day when Tyler was eleven years old, when they were standing in line at the bank, his mother asked him if he was gay. Tyler said that he was. Tyler's mother was not surprised. She had thought that he might be gay for quite a while. She and Tyler's stepfather Ken were accepting, but Tyler feared that his biological father and stepmother would not be accepting if they knew. So Tyler decided to hold off telling them for as long as possible.

Even though Oakley did not feel ready to be openly gay in his school or community, he yearned to find a place where he could express his true self outside of the family. At that time, a website called Myspace was one of the most popular social networking platforms. Many people were setting up pages where they could blog, share photos and videos, and make new friends. One day, Oakley set up a page on Myspace where he felt that he could be

INTERNET SAFETY

While the internet provides many wonderful opportunities for entertainment, information, and connection, it is also a place where predators, scammers, and others with bad intentions lurk.

If you meet someone in person, you can often tell their age and if they are male or female. But on the internet, people can pretend to be whoever they want others to think they are. A fifty-year-old man who is looking for children or teens to victimize can easily find a photo of a boy or girl and pretend to be a kid of the same age as the children he wants to prey on. He can view his intended victim's profile, find out all about his or her interests, and pretend he likes the same things. He does this to win young people's trust. Social media websites try their best to block people with bad intentions. But unfortunately, this usually doesn't happen until someone reports them.

When teens go online, do not use your full name or address. Also, do not tell anyone, even people at your school, what username and password you use. Giving your username and password to a friend might seem harmless. But if that person passes that information to others, they can use your username and password to post messages and pictures that could get you into trouble.

If you are LGBTQ+, the internet is a great place to find support. But until you are ready to come out to everyone you know, it is best not to use your real name online. Google and other internet search engines make it easy for anyone who is curious to type your name in a search engine and see what you have posted on the internet. If you decide to make internet posts about anything you want to keep private, it is best not to use your real name.

himself without having to worry about other people's judgments or be harassed.

When he filled out the user profile, he came to a question that asked if he was interested in men or women. Oakley decided to type "men." Tyler had not yet come out to his biological father, but he did not think that his biological father was likely to read anything he wrote on his Myspace page.

During his career as a YouTube vlogger, Tyler Oakley has won many honors and awards. Here he is accepting the Streamy 2014 Entertainer of the Year Award.

TYLER'S BIOLOGICAL FATHER FINDS OUT

One day, someone who attended the same church as Tyler's biological father was on the internet and came across Tyler's Myspace page. He read where Tyler posted that he was interested in men and told Tyler's biological father. One day, Tyler's biological father surprised him by inviting him to lunch. Almost as soon as Tyler arrived, his biological father asked Tyler about the Myspace page. Tyler confirmed that yes, that was his Myspace page and yes, he was gay.

Tyler's father was worried and upset. He had conservative religious views and believed that being gay was a sin. He pushed for Tyler to go to "conversion therapy" because he thought it

CONVERSION THERAPY

Conversion therapy is a controversial and unscientific practice of trying to change someone's sexual orientation from homosexual or bisexual to heterosexual. Some conservative religious organizations encourage parents to put children or teens who are gay, lesbian, bisexual, or transgender into conversion therapy programs, where psychological and spiritual methods are used in an attempt to change their sexual orientation or gender identity. Conversion therapy is sometimes called reparative therapy. The American Psychiatric Association is against the practice of conversion therapy. Psychological experts have stated that there is no solid evidence that any of the methods used in conversion therapy can change a person's sexual orientation.

The American Academy of Child and Adolescent Psychiatry (AACAP) wrote in their 2018 report *The AACAP Policy on Conversion Therapies:*

> The American Academy of Child and Adolescent Psychiatry finds no evidence to support the application of any "therapeutic intervention" operating under the premise that a specific sexual orientation, gender identity, and/or gender expression is pathological. Furthermore, based on the scientific evidence, the AACAP asserts that such conversion therapies (or other interventions imposed with the intent of promoting a particular sexual orientation and/or gender as a preferred outcome) lack scientific credibility and clinical utility. Additionally, there is evidence that such interventions are harmful. As a result, conversion therapies should not be part of any behavioral health treatment of children and adolescents.

In addition to not being effective in changing a person's sexual orientation or gender identity, conversion therapy has been known to cause anxiety, depression, and suicide attempts. Because of the potential harm these methods can cause, some states in the United States and other countries have banned conversion therapy.

would change Tyler from being gay. Tyler refused. When his biological father continued to push the issue, Tyler told him that he liked being the person he was and had no interest in being straight, or heterosexual.

After Tyler's biological father found out he was gay, their relationship became more strained than it had been before. Because his biological father could not accept the fact that his son was gay, Tyler tried to spend as little time as he could with him.

Nearly a decade later, Tyler's biological father started to soften his attitude. When Tyler saw that his biological father was being more accepting, he and his biological father started to grow closer. In a 2018 article by Jess Cagle for *People* magazine, Tyler said, "I'm really glad that I was patient with him. I'm really glad that he took time and put in the effort, because for a lot of parents I don't think it's that easy right off the bat."

CHAPTER TWO

Teen Years Bring New Challenges

A s Oakley entered his teen years, he had openly gay teachers and classmates. Still, he did not feel secure enough to come out at school. He knew that sometimes teens who come out as LGBTQ+ are bullied, and he didn't want to do anything that might cause his life to become more difficult than it already was.

BATTLING EATING DISORDERS

Oakley thought that getting rid of his extra weight would make him feel better and be more popular at school. So he decided to take action. In addition to severely limiting the amount of food he ate, Oakley went to the gym before school nearly every day to exercise. By the time he was in seventh grade, Oakley had lost 30 pounds (14 kilograms). However, he was having a serious battle with anorexia. In a 2017 interview with *Attitude* magazine, Oakley said, "It was a time when I was unsure about myself and insecure. I would look at myself, based on my size, or how I looked, and I would see this disconnect. I thought I was unlovable, and not just to others, but to myself."

Since Tyler Oakley was a small child, he loved to be on stage and entertain people. His love of entertaining helped him find success as a YouTube vlogger.

MUSIC AND DRAMA

A teacher at the school Oakley attended, Ms. Borton, realized that Oakley was not only underweight, but unhappy and anxious. She became concerned about Oakley and took time to talk to him at every opportunity. Ms. Borton taught choir and encouraged Oakley to participate in the school choir, musicals, and plays. Oakley found that he enjoyed having the opportunity to express himself in these activities, as well as make new friends who shared his interests. Oakley also decided to join the school's yearbook committee.

TEENS AND EATING DISORDERS

The pressure to have what others consider to be a perfect body is everywhere. Television, magazines, movies, and advertisements push the idea that if you want to be happy and successful, you must be thin and good looking. As unrealistic as these images are, the desire to conform to the Hollywood image of beauty makes many people, especially teenagers, feel that their weight, body shape, or other things about their appearance are not good enough.

The pressure to conform to unattainable standards is a major reason that teens develop eating disorders. It is estimated that one or two out of every one hundred teens in America struggle with eating disorders. The two major eating disorders are anorexia and bulimia.

People who have anorexia fear they will gain weight if they eat normal meals and often have a distorted sense of their actual size. They eat as little as possible and often exercise obsessively. Sometimes, their weight becomes dangerously low before they or their family seek professional help.

Bulimia is another common eating disorder. The major difference is that while people with anorexia eat very little, people with bulimia often eat a lot, also known as bingeing, then make themselves throw up to prevent weight gain. As with anorexia, people with bulimia sometimes become dangerously underweight before they seek help.

A 2018 article by Heather Monroe in *US News and World Report* revealed how serious of a problem eating disorders can be. The article states:

Diagnoses of eating disorders, specifically anorexia nervosa, carry the highest death rate of all mental health disorders. This is due in part to the higher-than-average rate of suicide among those with eating disorders, and partly to the medical complications associated with eating disorders. Adolescents are among those at the greatest risk, as the most common age of onset for eating disorders is between 12 and 25.

Eating disorders, such as anorexia and bulimia, can cause serious health problems, such as malnutrition, and can even lead to death. Often, professional help is required to overcome them.

While Oakley was still battling his eating disorder, these activities gave him something to focus on besides food. By the time Oakley was in ninth grade, he had his eating disorder under control. Still, he had to struggle with issues around body image.

When Oakley was fourteen, the age at which youth in Michigan could legally work at the time, he got a job at Arby's. That gave him a steady income and something positive to focus on.

Tyler Oakley uses his platform as a YouTube star to help spread acceptance of and understanding about the LGBTQ+ community and the issues they face.

GETTING OUTED

When Oakley was in high school, he developed a crush on one of his male friends. He had not yet come out. Oakley wanted his friend to know, but at the same time, he was afraid to tell him because he was pretty sure that his friend was straight. Also, Oakley feared that if his friend knew he had a crush on him, it might wreck the friendship. One day, Oakley told a trusted female friend his secret and made her promise not to tell anyone. But instead of keeping Oakley's crush a secret, she went to the boy and told him. Oakley was afraid the boy would want nothing to do with him once he knew, but they remained friends. After that, Oakley gradually started to come out to people he trusted at school.

Despite the struggles he was going through, Oakley had many good relationships and good feelings about his high school and the experiences he had during his time there. After Oakley became famous, he went back to visit his school and surprised the students and teachers. He even made a video about the trip and posted it on his YouTube channel.

CHAPTER THREE

College and Early YouTube Years

A fter Oakley graduated from high school, he enrolled at Michigan State University. At first, he considered a career in teaching. But later, he decided to study for a career in marketing and communication.

YouTube is a popular internet platform for people like Tyler Oakley who want their videos to reach a wide audience.

Even though Oakley enjoyed his new experiences at college, he missed his three best friends from high school. Oakley had heard about a website called YouTube, where people could upload videos and share them with their friends and family. Oakley had just saved up to buy a laptop computer, so he decided to give YouTube a try.

EARLY YEARS OF YOUTUBE

YouTube was founded by Chad Hurley, Steve Chen, and Jawed Karam, three men in their twenties who worked for PayPal. They came up with the idea after they were unable to upload and share a video they shot at a dinner party. They realized that if they needed a website where they could upload and share videos, other people probably did, too. After buying a domain name and setting up the technology, they uploaded their first video on April 23, 2005. It was a video of Karam talking to an elephant at the zoo. Word about this new video sharing website quickly spread.

By August 2005, YouTube had around seven thousand users and more than one hundred thousand video views a day. Several months later, *PC World* named YouTube one of the top ten best products of 2006. At the time, the content on YouTube was very different from what you see there today. It was used mostly for posting funny animal videos, videos of family events, and short clips of television shows.

On December 25, 2006, *Time* named "You" as the person of the year in recognition of the user-generated content people were posting on internet services such as Facebook, YouTube, and Myspace. In 2007, YouTube started a Featured Videos section on its home page where the company posted videos they thought deserved a large audience. YouTube also has categories for Most Viewed and Most Subscribed videos.

At the time, most people who posted videos on YouTube did not have high-tech equipment. Many just used the camera and microphone in their computer. But even without advanced lighting and the high-definition cameras today's star vloggers use, YouTube provided a perfect platform for future stars like Tyler Oakley to develop a following.

OAKLEY STARTS A YOUTUBE CHANNEL

Oakley posted his first videos on YouTube in 2007, during his freshman year at Michigan State University. Oakley's first video, posted on September 18, 2007, was a ten-minute tour of his dorm room. In many of his early videos, Oakley talked about things that were going on in his life. One day, he realized that one hundred people were watching his videos. At that point, he knew that people other than his family and friends were watching. He continued to post videos on a regular basis, taking about life, school, pop culture, and other things he was interested in.

Oakley soon learned the value of collaboration. One of his early YouTube collaborations was to produce a weekly video for the 5AwsomeGays YouTube channel, a collaboration between himself and a group of LGBTQ+ vloggers that ran from 2008 to 2011.

When Tyler Oakley was a student at Michigan State University, he studied marketing and communications. The knowledge he gained there helped him succeed on YouTube.

In 2008, Oakley decided to make a video praising the Trevor Project for the work they did to help LGBTQ+ teens and young adults who were considering suicide find hope and reasons to live. The video was featured on YouTube's home page on Charity Day. That video brought many new viewers to Oakley's YouTube channel.

BREAKUP AND DEPRESSION

While Oakley was in college, he had his first serious boyfriend. But while Oakley was openly gay, his boyfriend was not. In 2008,

TREVOR PROJECT

The Trevor Project is a nonprofit organization that focuses on preventing suicide among LGBTQ+ youth. It was founded in West Hollywood, California, in 1998 by Peggy Rajski, Randy Stone, and James Lecesne.

Rajski, Stone, and Lecesne are the creators of an Academy Award winning film titled *Trevor* that was released in 1994. The film told the story of a thirteen-year-old boy who attempted to take his life because friends found out he was gay and bullied him. Before the film was scheduled to air on HBO in 1998, the creators realized that many LGBTQ+ teens who are being bullied might be watching the film, and there was no national hotline to help them. So they decided to take action. They formed the Trevor Project, an organization that would promote acceptance and support of LGBTQ+ youth and provide a twenty-four-hour-a-day, toll-free telephone hotline that people can call for help. The organization's first project, the

(CONTINUED ON THE NEXT PAGE)

(CONTINUED FROM THE PREVIOUS PAGE)

Because of their success in preventing LGBTQ+ suicide, The Trevor Project has always been one of Tyler Oakley's favorite organizations.

Trevor Lifeline, was funded by the Colin Higgins Foundation and the license fees that the group received from HBO in exchange for showing the film. The Trevor Project also works to advocate for LGBTQ+ youth and offers resources and trainings for those who want to help make sure LGBTQ+ youth feel safe in their schools and communities.

Through the years, many celebrities who are popular with teens and young adults have supported the Trevor Project through donations and endorsements of the group. These celebrities include Adam Lambert, Debra Messing, Elton John, Barack Obama, Ellen DeGeneres, Lady Gaga, Sigourney Weaver, and Tyler Oakley.

Oakley won a contest the Human Rights Campaign held with his National Coming Out Day video, and the prize was a trip to Washington, DC. Oakley was very excited about winning the award and looked forward to taking the trip. His boyfriend went with him, but when they were interviewed, he had to deny they had a relationship because he knew his boyfriend's aunt would hear about it. After that, their relationship started to go downhill and Oakley's boyfriend became abusive. Eventually, they broke up.

After the breakup, Oakley became depressed. For the first and only time in his life, he seriously considered suicide. Oakley called the Trevor Project hotline, and the counselor he talked with was able to help him. Because he had such a positive experience with The Trevor Project, Oakley decided to travel to California in 2010 and do a public relations internship with them. When Oakley became famous, the Trevor Project became the primary charity he promoted and did fundraising for.

CHAPTER FOUR

Jumping into Vlogging

After Oakley graduated from Michigan State University, he moved to San Francisco and took a job doing social media for a marketing company. While he enjoyed creating social media campaigns for the company, he hated having to wait through the long delays of the company's approval process.

OAKLEY'S VIDEOS START EARNING

While he was working for the social marketing company, Oakley continued making his own videos after he came home from his day job and posted them to his YouTube channel. From the beginning, Oakley decided to be openly gay on his YouTube vlogs. He loved having the opportunity to use his YouTube channel to talk about anything he wanted and be himself. Oakley liked to talk about things going on in his life, food, celebrities, and pop culture.

YouTube offered people who posted videos on their website the option of having ads come on before their videos in exchange for money. Like most young people, Oakley needed

As Tyler Oakley's video channel became more popular, he often took the opportunity to attend conventions and meet his fans in person.

all the money he could get, so he decided to monetize, or allow advertising, on his YouTube video channel.

As Oakley continued to post videos on his YouTube channel on a regular basis, more people started to watch, and his view numbers increased. The advertising that YouTube ran before Oakley's videos was starting to make money. This gave Oakley hope that one day, he might be able to leave the job he hated and have a career he loved as a YouTube vlogger.

As time went on, Oakley became increasingly frustrated with his day job. Working for the social media marketing company was taking up most of his time and energy. From what he knew about the company, Oakley felt he had little or no hope of this job leading to the kind of career he wanted.

BECOMING A FULL-TIME YOUTUBE VLOGGER

One day, Oakley made a bold but risky decision. He decided that he wanted to devote all his time to working on his video channel and quit his day job. The decision proved to be a good one. Only three years after he posted his first video, YouTube offered Oakley a national marketing campaign.

Tyler Oakley is openly gay and has worked to promote LGBTQ+ acceptance in schools as well as society.

By then, Oakley knew that many LGBTQ+ youth watched his YouTube channel and looked up to him. Many lived in areas where they had little or no support. While some of Oakley's videos were silly and about pop culture, he also made videos about more serious issues, such as eating disorders, harassment, and bullying against LGBTQ+ people.

During his early years on YouTube, Oakley received many messages that said he was the first gay person they had ever known. Many of those messages came from teens who lived in rural areas where there was

Because of his popularity as a YouTube celebrity, Tyler Oakley (*left*) has had the opportunity to meet and interview many famous people, including First Lady Michelle Obama (*second from left*).

little support for LGBTQ+ people, making it difficult to live as an openly gay person. In a 2014 interview with Lucas Grindley, writer for the *Advocate*, Oakley explained his video channel by saying, "It's not all about me being gay. It's kind of like an under-lying theme for me and is sprinkled throughout the videos."

MEETING CELEBRITIES

Oakley calls himself a "fangirl" and loves to talk about his favorite celebrities and pop culture. Eventually, some of the celebrities he talked about took notice. The music group One Direction

CAREERS IN VIDEO

When young people hear about YouTube celebrities, the money they make and the opportunities that fame on YouTube brings, many decide to start a YouTube channel of their own. Unfortunately, as with professional sports stars, music stars, actors, and others in the entertainment industry, only a small percentage of the people who try for fame are able to earn enough money to live on.

However, there are many careers where you can be involved in video production. These careers include camera operator, video editor, video script writer, and director. While some people who like to do video work use freelance websites to find people in need of their skills, more permanent video-related jobs can also be found at television stations, advertising agencies, in education, government, and many other places.

While making videos to post on YouTube might not bring you fame and fortune, you can still have fun and gain experience in all areas of video work by starting a YouTube channel of your own.

heard what a big fan Oakley was of their work and agreed to let him interview them for his vlog. He also interviewed many other famous people, such as Darren Criss from *Glee*, President Barack Obama, and First Lady Michelle Obama. In 2013, Oakley had an opportunity to do voice acting when he performed the voice of Mr. McNeely in the comedy web series *The Most Popular Girls in School*. Opportunities like that brought even more subscribers to Oakley's channel. In 2013, Oakley's YouTube channel reached the amazing milestone of one million subscribers.

GENERATION LIKE

As Oakley's YouTube channel grew, more people began to take notice. Oakley was one of the main YouTube vloggers featured on a 2014 episode of the PBS series *Frontline*. The episode was titled "Generation Like" and it explored the internet and YouTube culture, as well as how big-name brands were using Facebook, YouTube, and other social media sites where "likes" were important to interact with teens. At the time "Generation Like" was filmed, Oakley had approximately five million followers on his YouTube channel. The exposure Oakley received from this documentary prompted even more people to watch his videos.

By the time "Generation Like" was filmed, Oakley was already getting so many offers from companies that wanted to pay for him to promote their products that he was able to pick and choose the companies he wanted to partner with. His sponsors included Taco Bell, Pepsi, Audible, and other big-name companies that wanted to connect with Oakley's fans.

After "Generation Like" aired, Oakley sent *Frontline* a message saying, "I see tweets all the time from people all over who have seen me on the program. Whether it's from being shown in a classroom or it was shown for the first time in Australia a few weeks ago, it's always reaching new audiences and they're letting me know."

CHAPTER FIVE

Fame Brings New Opportunities

Tyler Oakley's fame has led to important opportunities, including a book deal and a starring role in the documentary film *Snervous*, which he talks about here.

As Oakley gained more fans and his YouTube channel grew, mainstream media outlets started reaching out to him. Soon, he was getting opportunities he had never dreamed of when he started his channel. Oakley was invited to appear on *The Amazing Race*, *The Ellen Show*, *Larry King Now*, *Fear Factor*, and many other television shows. He was also featured in magazines such as *Forbes*, *Time*, *Out*, and *Advocate*. In 2015, Oakley became a published author when Simon and Shuster published a book of his humorous personal essays titled *Binge*.

TYLER OAKLEY'S SLUMBER PARTY

In 2014, Oakley decided to get out from behind the video camera for a while and tour with a live, on-stage show. He called his live stage show "Tyler Oakley's Slumber Party." Oakley brought his longtime friend and YouTube vlogger Korey Khul on tour to be part of the events. The two, as well as many of the teens who came to watch the show, wore oversized onesie pajamas. Oakley also brought his mother, who was known as Queen Jackie from appearances in Oakley's videos, onstage to participate in the fun.

Some of the stops along the tour, as well as Oakley's day-to-day life during that time, were filmed by a company called the Awesomness Films production company. The documentary was titled *Snervous*, after a word Oakley made up that means being both scared and nervous. *Snervous* was released in

In 2016, Tyler Oakley took home the Best Web Personality award at the 20th Annual Webby Awards in New York City.

2015. It was shown in limited release in theaters and can now be watched on streaming services.

During that time, Oakley was also appearing at YouTube-inspired conventions where fans come to meet their favorite YouTube stars. While Oakley enjoyed touring and meeting his fans, there were things he found challenging about the tour and conventions. Sometimes he was mobbed by large groups of fans because there were not enough security people to control the crowd. Also, at public events, Oakley was not able to be in control of everything that happened, as he was used to doing when he recorded and edited videos before posting them on YouTube.

RAISING FUNDS FOR THE TREVOR PROJECT

Oakley's fame also brought him more opportunities to help LGBTQ+ youth. He held fundraisers for the Trevor Project. Oakley decided to use his YouTube channel to raise funds for the Trevor Project for the first time in 2013. Instead of sending him birthday gifts, Oakley asked his YouTube fans to donate to the Trevor Project. Oakley was celebrating his twenty-fourth birthday, so his goal was to raise $24,000 during the month of March. Oakley's YouTube viewers answered his call for donations, and he soon exceeded his fundraising goal and his donation total was approximately $29,000.

Suicide is a serious risk for LGBTQ+ youth. A 2015 survey by the Centers for Disease Control and Prevention revealed that 34.9 percent of lesbian, gay, bisexual, and questioning youth were considering suicide seriously, and 24 percent had attempted suicide in the past year. By contrast, 14.8 percent of straight youth were considering suicide and 6.3 percent had attempted suicide in the past year.

Every year, Oakley uses his birthday as a fundraising event for the Trevor Project. Since his first fundraiser in 2013, he has raised a total of over one million dollars for the Trevor Project. He also hosted the pre–award ceremony red carpet events for the Trevor Project and participated in other projects for the organization. In 2014, Oakley won the Trevor Project's Youth Innovator Award. The next day, Oakley posted on Instagram, "I share this award with you, my people - you're courageous enough to change the world and you inspire me every day."

Whatever he is doing, Tyler Oakley always brings his unique brand of humor and personality to a project.

MY CHOSEN FAMILY

While many of the videos Tyler Oakley posts to his YouTube channel are fun, he also takes on many serious topics. He has posted many videos about LGBTQ+ issues and the challenges LGBTQ+ youth can face in today's world.

Starting in June 2017, Oakley decided to post a video series titled My Chosen Family. In these videos, Oakley traveled around the country and interviewed people in the LGBTQ+ community about issues that affect their lives. These issues include adoption into LGBTQ+ families, LBGTQ+ refugees, bullying at school, and bridging the gap between youth and elders in the LGBTQ+ community.

Oakley told NBC News, "I have found just by making this series, there's so much I can learn and ways to be a better ally," he said. "If I want to be the best ally for disenfranchised people, it's not by speaking up for them. It's by letting them speak for themselves."

HELPING LGBTQ+ YOUTH FIND THEIR VOICE

Oakley believes that one of the best things about the internet and YouTube is that they offer unlimited opportunities for LGBTQ+ and other marginalized or misunderstood groups to communicate and connect. In a January 2017 interview with *Forbes* writer Natalie Robehmed, Oakley said, "When I was younger and still in the closet, I couldn't just Google 'coming-out story' to help me articulate what I was going through. YouTube provides a microphone for marginalized voices."

Even though Oakley is one of the most famous LGBTQ+ YouTube vloggers, he does not want to be viewed as the primary spokesperson for LGBTQ+ youth. Instead, he wants to help LGBTQ+ youth get their own voices onto the internet and other media. That is why in 2018, Oakley decided to partner with GLAAD's Rising Stars Grant Program. This program funds young LGBTQ+ content creators who use digital media or technology to put their voices, or the voices of other LGBTQ+ youth into the public space online or in their own communities.

When David Artavia, writer for *Advocate* magazine, asked Oakley about the winners of the 2018 GLAAD Rising Star Grant Program, Oakley replied:

> They are storytellers, and they're politicians, and they're artists, and they're leaders and students; and for all of them—they're queer and they're iconic in their own ways… When I met these young people, I felt like I was meeting the future leaders of HRC and GLAAD and GLSEN. I was meeting the people that are going to lead movements … and I felt like the future is bright.

LOOKING TO THE FUTURE

Whatever Oakley does in the future, his YouTube channel will likely remain his focal point. That is where Oakley comes to chat with his fans and report on things that are going on in his life. As of now, Oakley has not commented on his future plans. But whatever he decides to do, it will likely be amazing!

TIMELINE

1989 Tyler Oakley is born in Jackson, Michigan.

2007 Oakley uploads his first video to YouTube in 2007 while a freshman at Michigan State University.

2010 Oakley travels to California to intern for the Trevor Project and a public relations firm.

2011 Oakley cohosts the Trevor Project's red carpet event, Trevor LIVE.

2013 Tyler Oakley's YouTube channel reaches one million subscribers. Oakley performs the voice of Mr. McNeely in the comedy web series *The Most Popular Girls in School.* Oakley raises $29,000 for the Trevor Project during his first online birthday fundraiser.

2014 Oakley is featured in the *Frontline* investigative report "Generation Like."

2015 Oakley's book of humorous personal essays, *Binge,* is published. Oakley interviews First Lady Michelle Obama about the importance of education. Oakley starts cohosting a new podcast, *Psychobabble*, with his friend Korey Kuhl.

2016 Oakley is listed in *Hollywood Reporter*'s Top 25 Digital Stars. Oakley is listed in *Out* magazine's Power 50.

2018 Oakley wins *Out* magazine's Power of Originality Award. Oakley wins the Visibility Award from the Human Rights Campaign.

GLOSSARY

advocate To openly support or recommend something.

anorexia A disorder that causes people to have an obsessive desire to lose weight.

brand The recognizable identity or image of a product or service.

bulimia An eating disorder where people binge and throw up to lose weight.

collaboration Working with others toward a common goal.

conversion therapy The unscientific practice of trying to change a person's sexual orientation from gay, lesbian, or bisexual to straight (heterosexual).

disenfranchised Deprived of the privileges or rights others have.

entrepreneur A person who takes a risk to start and operate a business.

fangirl A person who has an obsessive interest in celebrities, movies, TV shows, etc.

followers People who track someone's posts on YouTube or other social media websites.

internship A paid or unpaid starter position in a business or organization for a student or trainee.

LGBTQ+ Describing a person who is lesbian, gay, bisexual, transgender, or questioning or queer.

likes In social media, the number of viewers that indicate they like something that was posted on social media.

marginalized Describing individuals or groups of people who are treated as inferior or insignificant.

marketing Promoting and selling products or services.

out To reveal that someone is LGBTQ+ without their permission.

pop culture Popular entertainment that is enjoyed by a large percentage of the population.

role model Someone others respect and look up to.

social media Websites and other online applications that allow users to create content and share it with others.

subscribers People who automatically receive updates from people, organizations, or businesses that post on social media.

trajectory The path something follows as it moves forward.

upload To send data, such as videos, to a website on the internet.

visibility How well something or someone can be seen.

vlog A video blog.

vlogger A person who posts video blogs, especially on YouTube.

FOR MORE INFORMATION

GLAAD
5455 Wilshire Boulevard, #1500
Los Angeles, CA 90036
(323) 933-2240
Website: http://www.glaad.org
Facebook, Instagram, and
    Twitter: @glaad
GLAAD has been working for
    the acceptance of LGBTQ+
    individuals since 1985.
    Their work includes push-
    ing for antidiscrimination
    laws and public education
    about issues that affect the
    LGBTQ+ community.

GLSEN
110 William Street, 30th Floor
New York, NY 10038
(212) 727-0135
Website: https://www.glsen.org
Facebook: @GLSEN and
    @gaystraightalliances
Instagram and Twitter: @glsen
This organization helps create
    safe, affirming schools for
    K–12 LGBTQ+ students,
    where they can thrive without
    having to deal with bullying
    and harassment. It offers
    resources for starting and

running gay-straight alliances
at schools.

Human Rights Campaign
1640 Rhode Island Avenue NW
Washington, DC 20036-3278
(800) 777-4723
Website: https://www.hrc.org
Facebook and Instagram:
    @humanrightscampaign
Twitter: @HRC
The Human Rights Campaign
    is the largest LGBT civil
    rights group in the United
    States. They work to ensure
    and expand civil rights for
    LGBT people.

LGBT Youth Allies
Website: http://www.youthallies
    .com
Facebook: @LGBTYouthAllies
Twitter: @youthallies
This project supports LGBT
    youth, as well as their families
    and allies. It provides a list
    of links to organizations
    and resources.

LGBT Youth Line
PO Box 73118, Wood Street PO

Toronto, ON M4Y 2W5
Canada
(416) 962-2232
Website: http://www.youthline.ca
Facebook, Twitter, and Insta-
    gram: @lgbtyouthline
LGBT Youth Line is a youth-
    led organization that helps
    LGBT and Two-Spirit youth in
    Ontario through anonymous
    peer support, resources,
    and training.

**National Eating Disorders
    Association**
1500 Broadway
Suite 1101
New York, NY 10036
(800) 931-2237
Website: https://www
    .nationaleatingdisorders.org
Facebook: @NationalEatingDis-
    ordersAssociation
Instagram: @neda
Twitter: @NEDAstaff
This association assists indi-
    viduals and families that are
    dealing with eating disor-
    ders, provides information on
    eating disorders, and runs an
    eating disorders helpline.

Positive Space Network
504 Iroquois Shore Road, Unit
    12A

Oakville, ON
Canada
(905) 878-9785
Website: https://www
    .positivespacenetwork.ca
Facebook:
    @positivespacenetworkCA
Twitter: @PSN_HALTON
Instagram: @PSN.HALTON
The network provides educa-
    tion, awareness, visibility,
    and support programs for
    LGBTQ+ youth and spon-
    sors a twenty-four-hour-a-day
    crisis hotline.

The Trevor Project
PO Box 69232
West Hollywood, CA 90069
(866) 488-7386
Website: https://www
    .thetrevorproject.org
Facebook: @TheTrevorProject
Twitter and Instagram:
    @trevorproject
The Trevor Project provides
    a crisis and suicide pre-
    vention hotline for LGBT
    youth. It also provides a
    judgment-free community
    for LGBT youth to talk, text,
    and form community in their
    online social space.

FOR FURTHER READING

Birley, Shane. *How to Be a Blogger and Vlogger in 10 Easy Lessons.* Lake Forest, CA: Walter Foster Jr., 2016.

Furgang, Adam. *20 Great Career-Building Activities Using YouTube.* New York, NY: Rosen Publishing, 2017.

Hall, Kevin. *Creating and Building Your Own YouTube Channel.* New York, NY: Rosen Central, 2017.

Hand, Carol. *Getting Paid to Produce Videos.* New York, NY: Rosen Publishing, 2017.

Kyncl, Robert, and Maany Peyvan. *Streampunks: YouTube and the Rebels Remaking Media.* New York, NY: HarperBusiness, 2017.

Loh-Hagan, Virginia. *YouTube Channel.* Ann Arbor, MI: 45th Parallel Press, 2017.

Oakley, Tyler. *Binge.* New York, NY: Simon & Schuster Ltd, 2016.

Paul, Harriet, Caroline Rowlands, and Gideon Summerfield. *The Vloggers Yearbook.* New York, NY: Little Bee Books/Simon & Schuster, 2015.

Putnam, Will, and We the Unicorns. *Vlogging 101: The Ultimate Guide to Becoming a YouTuber.* London, UK: Studio Press, 2017.

Staley, Erin. *Vloggers and Vlogging.* New York, NY: Rosen Publishing, 2017.

BIBLIOGRAPHY

American Academy of Child and Adolescent Psychiatry (AACAP). "Conversion Therapy. Approved by Council February 2018." https://www.aacap.org/AACAP/Policy_Statements/2018/Conversion_Therapy.aspx.

Artavia, David. "Matthew Shepard, Tyler Oakley: Lives Separated by Two Decades of Change" *Advocate*, September 24, 2018. https://www.advocate.com/youth/2018/9/24/matt-shepard-tyler-oakley-lives-separated-two-decades-change.

Attitude. "Tyler Oakley Opens Up About Eating Disorder Battle in Attitude's May Issue." March 29, 2017. https://attitude.co.uk/article/tyler-oakley-opens-up-about-eating-disorder-battle-in-attitudes-may-issue/13984.

Biography.com. "Tyler Oakley Biography." A&E Television Networks, December 5, 2017. https://www.biography.com/people/tyler-oakley-12517.

Brammer, John Paul. "Tyler Oakley's New 'Chosen Family' Series Spotlights LGBTQ+ Resilience." NBC, June 20, 2017. https://www.nbcnews.com/feature/nbc-out/tyler-oakley-s-new-chosen-family-series-spotlights-lgbtq-resilience-n774561.

Cagle, Jess. "Tyler Oakley on Coming Out to His Conservative Father: 'I'm Really Glad I Was Patient with Him.'" *People*, March 8, 2018. https://people.com/movies/tyler-oakley-on-coming-out-to-his-conservative-father-im-really-glad-i-was-patient-with-him.

Carrasco, Ed. "Tyler Oakley: Growing the LGBT YouTube Community and Supporting the Trevor Project." New Media, June 29, 2013. http://newmediarockstars.com/2013/06/tyler-oakley-growing-the-lgbt-youtube-community-and-supporting-the-trevor-project-proudtolove-youtube-creator-series.

Christensen, Jen. "LGBQ Teens Face Serious Suicide Risk, Research Finds." CNN, December 19, 2017. https://www.cnn.com/2017/12/19/health/lgbq-teens-suicide-risk-study/index.html.

Ellis-Petersen, Hannah. "Tyler Oakley: Popular Champion of the YouTube Confessional." *The Guardian*, November 8, 2015. https://www.theguardian.com/technology/2015/nov/08/tyler-oakley-popular-champion-of-the-youtube-confessional.

Fallon, Kevin. "It's Time to Take Tyler Oakley Seriously." The Daily Beast, September 17, 2015. https://www.thedailybeast.com/its-time-to-take-tyler-oakley-seriously.

Gomez, Patrick. "Inside Tyler Oakley's Unlikely Rise to Fame and Fortune." *People*, May 2, 2017. https://people.com/social-media-stars/tyler-oakley-youtube-bio-fame-fortune.

Grindley, Lucas. "Tyler Oakley Could Be the First Gay Person You Ever Met." *Advocate*, July 30, 2014. https://www.advocate.com/40-under-40-emerging-voices/2014/07/30/40-under-40-tyler-oakley-could-be-first-gay-person-you-ever.

Kuehler, M. "Inspiration from Tyler Oakley, Role Model." UTimes, January 12, 2018. https://medium.com/@UTimes2017/inspiration-from-tyler-oakley-role-model-88c99ef6866d.

Lavelle, Moria. "What Did 'Generation Like' Think of 'Generation Like'?" PBS.org, August 5, 2014. https://www.pbs.org/wgbh/frontline/article/what-did-generation-like-think-of-generation-like.

Monroe, Heather. "The Truth About Teen Eating Disorders." *U.S. News and World Report*, January 4, 2018. https://health.usnews.com/health-care/for-better/articles/2018-01-04/the-truth-about-teen-eating-disorders.

Moore, Chadwick. "Tyler Oakley and the Cult of Oversharing." *Out*, February 5, 2015. https://www.out.com/entertainment/2015/2/05/tyler-oakley-and-cult-oversharing.

Oakley, Tyler (@tyleroakley. "Last night I received the Trevor Youth Innovator Award)from @trevorproject. I share this award with you, my people - you're courageous enough to change the world and you inspire me every day." Instagram post, June 17, 2014. https://www.instagram.com/p/pWOOGDt_2w.

On Top magazine staff. "Tyler Oakley: Lack of Positive Queer Representation Made Me Fear Coming Out Gay." *On Top* magazine, October 27, 2018. http://www.ontopmag.com/article/45340/Tyler_Oakley_Lack_Of_Positive_Queer_Representation_Made_Me_Fear_Coming_Out_Gay.

Robehmed, Natalie. "30 Under 30 Hollywood: Tyler Oakley, Margot Robbie, Evan Rachel Wood and the Class of 2017." *Forbes*, January 3, 2017. https://www.forbes.com/sites/natalierobehmed/2017/01/03/30-under-30-hollywood-margot-robbie-tyler-oakley-evan-rachel-wood-and-the-class-of-2017.

Spangler, Tod. "Tyler Oakley Launches LGBTQ Event Series on YouTube for Pride Month." *Variety*, June 19, 2018. https://variety.com/2018/digital/news/tyler-oakley-lgbtq-series-youtube-pride-month-pins-1202850640.

INDEX

ABOUT THE AUTHOR

Anita Louise McCormick is the author of many books. Her previous titles for Rosen Publishing include *Rosa Parks and the Montgomery Bus Boycott* (Spotlight on the Civil Rights Movement), *The Native American Struggle in United States History*, and *Everything You Need to Know About Nonbinary Gender Identities* (The Need to Know Library). McCormick identifies as nonbinary and is enthusiastic about working to increase public awareness and understanding of issues facing LGBTQ+ youth.

PHOTO CREDITS